Paddy is Fo~~ckin Dyin~~
Quite Sick!

MURPHY IN MIAMI

A Comic Adult Poem
By J.J. Barrett

Published by The Dub Press
Amber, Violet-Hill,
Bray,
Co. Wicklow,
Ireland.

British Library Cataloguing in Publication Data.
A catalogue record for this book is available from the British Library.

ISBN 0-9527923-7-0

Typesetting, design and printing by Kingdom Printers Limited

CONTENTS

Note: There is no resemblance or relationship to anybody living or dead and this book is purely fictional.

INTRODUCTION TO PADDY MURPHY

Paddy Murphy is the epitome of Irish bachelorhood. More especially in some snug little rural area of Kerry. He is 39 years old and has been at that age for at least ten years now. He is a strong six feet tall, and though losing his hair fairly rapidly, and weighing in at fourteen and three quarter stone, he could be considered attractive enough to some women. Especially where they outnumber men ten to one.

Paddy has a conservative line in clothes but can be very adventurous and even outrageous when confronted with things unknown and places totally new to him. Moreover after drink. He seldom sees danger and after a lifetime of Junior Hurling Matches and some pub brawls he can take care of himself admirably. Like all Kerrymen he enjoys a joke and good conversation or even the odd verse, more especially, in the pub, where he spends a great deal of his waking hours. While on this point may it be stated that Paddy's affection for the Irish National Brew, is very close indeed, with his daily intake of ten to fifteen pints. Or as Paddy would put it "A couple of Gallons".

On Sundays and Holy Days this number would rise to three or more Gallons depending on which Mass Paddy attended before going to the Pub. His presence at Mass is more abstract than real as he has not entered the Church since his Mother's Funeral.

He stands outside the back door where he chats with some friends until the signal of the "Peace be with You" when he shakes hands with his few companions outside the door and leads them away to the Pub, asking them what they'll have as they walk out the Chapel Yard. "Still", he says, "I would hate like Hell to miss Mass – Sunday would not be the same without it".

Paddy Murphy is a Farmer, according to himself, though he hasn't farmed since his Mother's Funeral over twenty years ago. The day she died he leased out the land to a more careful and industrious neighbour.

So now can you see that Paddy has few needs and no wants. Life can be lived as he sees fit. He lives alone, without brother or sister, kith or kin. Has enough money to buy his ample ration of Porter and has enough left over to put a bit aside for his "Burial Fund", as he calls his savings.

Paddy hasn't too much interest in women and describes anyone who prefers women to drink as Queer. Paddy got planning permission for some of his land but that failed when his Bank Manager took back the umbrella. Last year he took to watching "Miami Vice" on the television in the pub, and one night after Ten Pints of Porter, Paddy decided to cash in the "Burial Fund" and go to Miami for the very first holiday of his life.

PADDY MEETS A BANKER

Come in Paddy Murphy
Mo grá mo stór.
With your planning permission
You're welcome for sure.
I'll give you whatever
You need or like,
To build twenty or fifty
Houses, buy a
brand new bike.

It's damp outside
And, I'm afraid you'll
get wet.
So, here's an umbrella,
My friend, my pet.
My great, loyal customer,
My golfing friend.
You spread jobs around,
Yes, I'm with you 'till the end.

Oh! 'twas a hurricane instead
I read it wrong, so,
I'm not to be found,
'twas the final gong.
The Banker retired,
With pension grand
So Paddy decided to
Try his hand
In Florida for a while.

PADDY MEETS A MOSQUITO IN MIAMI

One night in Miami
After Ten Pints of Porter
Paddy stopped near some bushes
To pass his water.
But Honest to God
'Tis a terrible thing
To meet a little "hoor"
With a dreadful sting.

For it seems as Paddy
Produced his dick
The bloody mosquito
Was twice as quick
And diving down
With all his might
It landed poor Paddy
One Almighty bite.
With the speed of light
Paddy upped his zip.
His unfinished business

Left a bit of a drip.
Now 'tis a fearful, dreadful.
Terrifying thing,
If a man can't piss
Without fear of a sting.
What a male can discover
Between his fingers,
That because of a sting
His dick gets bigger
And looking down
In pained surprise
His member grows before his eyes.

And Lord above
Such a massive thing
Of which poor Paddy
Won't boast nor sing.
For larger though
His Dicky grows,
This helpless poor divil
Very well knows
His outrageous mickey
With horrible pain
Will not become
This size again.
Unless some night
Bursting with piss,
Paddy risks the passion
Of a mosquito's kiss.
Now 'tis truly sickening
And almost frightening
To reach such size
Without the real thing.

PADDY'S "MIAMI ADVICE"

One night in Miami
After ten pints of Porter
A black man
Asked Paddy
Is it a bit
Of a trick
To drink
All those pints
And would he
Never feel sick, in the morning?
So Paddy answered
As plain as
Could be
And he said
To the stranger
More advisedly.
If you understood me
I'm sure
You would see
If I did
Not feel sick
I'd think
There was
Something wrong
With me.
Now porter
Is porter
And sick

Is sick
But the
Worst I
Have felt
And tis a Terrible thing
Was to
Vomit until
I brought
Up the
Brown ring.

PADDY GOES FOR A MIDNIGHT SWIM

One Night in Miami
After ten pints of Porter
Paddy decided to
Enter some water.
He still doesn't
Know whether Porter or whim
Made him take
The plunge and go
For a swim.
What he didn't know
But learned later
Was that Miami
Is home for the Alligator.
Now his story could
Be very much worse
Were it not that
The "gator" missed
Paddy's arse
By inches.
Yes Fear is fear
When your'e in
The water
Being chased
By a hoor
Of an alligator.
The fright of God
Is a terrible thing
When you think

Your days have
Had their fling.
You never swam
So fast before
Trying like hell
To reach the shore.

His rounded body
Brave and stark
Was kicking harder
In the dark
Than ever before.
Paddy splashed
He roared for help
When those jaws
Made their effort
To take the shkelp.
Now 'tis often
In porter
Paddy will sing
Of the alligators efforts
To bight off his
Brown ring.

PADDY AT THE MEADOW

A day in the
Meadow was
Important indeed.
Through Winter
Days it provided
The feed
For the animals
He kept
Upon the farm.
Now work
Was warm
And days
Were long.
The neighbours
Cored, and with
Fun and song
They helped
Each other to
Save the hay
No man
Or woman
Counted hours
Or pay.
So one
Summer morning in
The month
Of May
Paddy's mother
Prepares food

For the day.
Paddy all
Muscle, with
Healthy tan,
Looked a
Fine specimen
Of a man.
But much
To Paddy's
Mother's dismay
She had
Plenty of water
But no
Fist of Tay.   - at all
Paddy ran
Across a
Field to
Borrow some
Tay from
The widow
Drumm who,
Without chick
Or child,
Lived nearby.
The door
And half
Door were
Closed against
Him when
He got there
So Paddy
Being as

Friendly as ever
Lifted the
Latch or
The lever
Which opened
The top
Half of
The door.
His eyes
Like onions
Popped outside
His brow
Were showing
The shock
That came
Over him now.
For standing
There both
Stark and bare
Was the
Widow Drumm
Just drying
Her hair,
With a towel.
My mo,
Mother needs
A fisht
Of tay
To fill
The can
He began
To say.

Yerrah whisht
Said the
Widow, your'e
A terrible
Man, and
What is
Your hurry?
Leaning on
That half
Door starIng
At me.
Come in and
Sit upon
That chair
While I
Finish what
I'm doing
And I brush
My hair.
By the
God in
Heaven that
I adore
You would
Think you
Never saw before
A girl getting
Herself ready
So now
Sit down
Be nice
And steady

She had
Everything a
Man would need
And others
On which
A baby
Would feed.

As she
Glowed all over
A woman
More stately
Never upset
A man
So greatly
But honest
To God
I had
Terrible fear
With a pain
In my belly
An ache in
My groin
My heart
Palpitating
And I
Almost dyin,
Her shapely
White body
Looked so good
As she stood
Before me
A fully

Grown nude.
A pan
Of cold
Water upon
The table
To watch
Her washing
I just
Was not able
I knew
If another
Minute I'd stay
I'd run
The risk of
What neighbours
Might say.
Sure I
Only called
To borrow
Tay from
The widow,
To make
A sup,
When we'd
Get to
The meadow.
Now Irish
Weather can
Be so cruel
When you've
Hay on
The ground

You'd look
A fool
If to
Borrow tay
You called to
The widow
And had
Her on
The ground
Instead of
Hay on
The Meadow.
All that day
As we saved
The hay
I could hardly
Get her out
Of my head.
I must admit
To some regret
Whenever I'd
Look at the
Hay in
The shed.
Full to
The roof
With well
Saved hay,
The fruits
Of a lovely
Summers Day.
But then

My heart
Thumping
I'd find,
As my
Priorities
I'd unwind.
To think
Of the chance
I threw away
To make love
To the widow
Instead of loving
To make the hay.
I remembered
The way I
Shot for
The door
And I
Never got
So close
To a woman
Anymore
Until.

PADDY DESCRIBES MEETING AN EX NUN IN MIAMI

One night in Miami
After ten Pints
Of Porter
I met a girl
You'd have
To admire her.
She said
She was
An Ex-Nun
And she
Came to Miami
To Enjoy
The sun.
She reminded
Me of the
Widow Drumm
And she drank
A bottle of Whiskey
Before she'd come
Back to her Flat.
With me confused
Like I'd
Never been,
I gave myself
Up to this
Pretty Queen.
Though it's hard
To believe

She had been
A nun,
With all her tricks
You'd think
She invented fun.
I wished the lads
Could see me now
My greatest moment
Arrived, and, how
I'd do it
As advised
By all the boys
Both green
And wise
In Kelly's Pub
At home.
Then,
Like you'd peel
A banana she
Grabbed hold
Of me and
Opened her mouth
I got such a fright
Sure I gave
A terrible shout,
And raising her
Hair at the
Top of her head
I moved her clean
Up from the
Bottom of
The bed.

Oh that was
My favourite position
She said, but with
Teeth like hers
I was half afraid
For myself, and
The only way
That I knew how
Was the way at home
That they'd bull a cow
So she Turned off the Light.
This incident
Raised an
Undoubted spark and
I felt kind of
Good lyin
There in the dark.
She took my hand
Asking me to
Hold and
Caress her.
But though it
Being dark
I was still very shy,
And I suppose, I was
A bit of
A mother's boy.
So he hesitated
Find the thatch.
But got an idea
And asked for a match
Then he said

Would you mind
Standing out
On the floor
'Til I see
What I'm at
Then I'll know
For sure
And, of course
I will understand
Where you want
Me to place my hand
Well you'd
Never guess
What befell
This fine girl
As she stood
Out
Upon the floor.
Now, I being
So very green
Had to admit
I'd never seen
One so
Close yet.
And having warnings
From my friends
At home
A certain dose
To never catch.
The excitement was
Building up in me
So I ventured closer

With the match.
Not knowing much
About all this
I asked her
For a foreign kiss
So she pointed
Down with passion
And desire,
Then you had
Better do it fast
Because I think that
You're on fire
She said.
It was a close
Encounter and
He kept away
From women
Until he thought
The Lord above
Had him finally
Forgiven. Then!

PADDY AND THE ENEMA WITHIN

One night in Miami
After ten pints of Porter
As usual, Paddy
Had to pass his water
He selected a place
'Twas an iron gate
So Paddy unzipped
Sure relief was great.
But instead
Of relief
It was
Paddy's fate
To piss upon
An electrified gate.

Security men
Rushed from
All around
When they
Heard this
Indescribable sound
Of Paddy's
Agonising calls
For some
Kind soul
To release his balls
He roared
He screamed
At such

A pitch
'Til some
Decent man
Turned off
The switch.
As he
Lay there
Like smouldering turf
He felt quite tired
Of sun and surf
Of water full
Of alligators
And mosquito bites
Upon his creathur.
He vowed that
He would
No more roam
To foreign climes
So far
From home.
And pondering
On his frailty
He awaited
The ambulance
To casualty.

So Paddy
Was Eventually
Wheeled in.
After sirens
Had announced
With mournful din

That in
This wagon
Of smokey palls
Lay luckless Paddy
With bar-b-qued Balls.

But after
Paddy had
A few
Nights sleep
He began to
Feel quite
Well again
Soon forgetting
Balls half roasted
And thinking
Of Porter by
The bucket.
The bright
Young Nurses
Were for sure
The unprescribed
But inevitable cure
For a man
Who had won
Many a battle
In hurling fields
And chasing cattle.
They all set out
To fix his ill
With curious flourish
And power at will.

Then one mischievous
Young lovely
Saw her chance
Advising Paddy
To remove
His Pants
So as fast
As you
Would cush
A duck,
With Paddy
Counting all
His luck
He almost kicked
His pants.
Out of
The place
And at
Her command
Turned on
His face.
He never
Had this
Thrill before
But did not
Know what
Was in store.
He thought
This lecherous
Lustful hunk
Was about
To score

Because he
Got drunk
And because
Of fate had
Pissed upon
An electrified gate.
But what
Happened next
In Florida
Was, Paddy got
Three pints
Of Enema.

PADDY TRIES TO BORROW A STOOL
IN MIAMI

You will have
To come back
Another day
Said the same suntanned
Nurse to Paddy Murphy.
We think your kidney
Is quite enlarged
And she flashed
A smile on the
Day he was
discharged
From Hospital.
He was a little confused
But trying to
Look cool.
For she told him
Come Monday
And bring his stool
And not to forget
His urine sample also.
That weekend
He worried a lot
Felt mixed up and
In a pickle
He knew all right
He'd have piss
For the bottle
But where in Miami

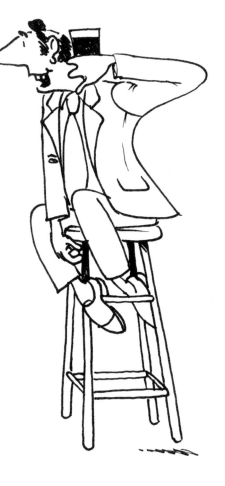

Would he borrow
A stool.
So he travelled
The bars
To and fro
Trying to Borrow
A stool for
A day or so
THEN SUNDAY NIGHT IN MIAMI
AFTER TEN PINTS OF PORTER
Paddy got a bottle
From a barman
To collect his water.
He mentioned his problem
About borrowing a stool
But the barmen explained
Nearly laughing a fit,
That the stool they needed
Was Paddy's shit.
But how in Heaven
Said Paddy with a curse,
Can I hand my
Shite to a pretty nurse
And how will I get
This to the Hospital?
After ten pints
Of Porter I'd
Need a large receptacle.
You only need
A little bit
Said the Barman
As if,

An expert on Shit.
So the
Following morning
The Miami sun
Saw Paddy
On busses
And people run.
For Paddy
Got on
With his
Urine sample
And his stool
Or shite
In a brown paper parcel.
Paddy is seldom
Very bashful
Or shy
And that was
The very reason why
He could not
Understand when
He went
Puce or purple
As so many people
Gave him such
A wide circle.
He smiled
He winked
Trying all
His charm
But he
Still had

The parcel
Under his arm.
When Paddy
Arrived at
The Hospital
He felt relieved
And even clever
As he handed up
The fruits of all
His endeavour.
That day
He boarded
A plane
For home
And I doubt
If from Ireland
He'll wander
Or roam
Except some night
After ten pints of Porter
He hungers for
Sand, Sex, Gators and Water.

MURPHY RIP.

And of course it
happened to this bloody man.
He was halfway across the Atlantic Ocean.
For Paddy diverted
his return flight plan.

Nobody will believe
it was all by chance but
Murphy landed
somewhere in France.
Where his past
came back to
haunt him most.
For de javu can
seem a ghost
He thought of
women from around
the world.
He had loved
With pride with
his flag
unfurled.
Then one night in Cannes after
ten pints of porter
Murphy had met a woman
Who really saw red.
When he stood on her rabbit
Getting out of her bed.

He was much travelled by then.
He met Monica in Monaco
And her brother Karlo
in Monte Carlo.
She was a terror to go
And he was, well,
don't you know.
It was eventually to be the end of poor Murphy!
There is a clinic in Lanzorote,
Where his stones were
quarried from near his botty.
Murphy's were cast into
The Atlantic calmly.
The result for South Florida
Being a huge tsunami.
He was just barely out when it happened.
This time he made
for home for sure.
Though in the quarry
department he was
two stones fewer.
The returned yank
felt as posh as golf.
Six months in the sun
with everything off.
In his shouped up chivic sure
He looked quite a toff.
Paddy raced towards
The slipway thinking it
was the 500 Indy.
His spoiler towards the wind,
he reversed through a doughnut.

Then into his wheelie and the
dark cold water of Dingle Bay, with Fungi.
Hey, hey, hey!
Can you fathom that?
Murphy was dead!!!
Did his many friends ullogoan
When that happened?
No!, not really, though almost.
They ululated instead.
Will there be ten pints
Of porter at Murphy's wake?
Not at all for Heaven's sake.
No! He wants no candles
Round his bed
No keening women
To recall what he said.
No priest or parson to
pray when he's dead.
No jersey or boots to
remind that he 'pled'
No Tricolour Flag to
Remind where he stood.
No beautiful woman
To say he was good.
No lover left to
boast what they did.
No rabbit under some
Beautie's bed. And
No poetry to scramble
His poor fucking head.

END